COMPLETING FORGIVENESS

Shirley Lamb

Shirley Lamb Ministries
1619 E 56th St • Tulsa, OK • (918) 747-1662

Scriptures are italicized with certain words underlined for emphasis by the author.

Dictionary definitions are taken from the <u>Random House College Dictionary</u>, Random House, Inc., 1975.

Cover design by Nancy Titolo

Original Edition:
HOW TO FORGIVE FROM YOUR HEART
Copyright ©1992 by Shirley Lamb
ISBN 0-9612364-1-8

Second Edition:
COMPLETING FORGIVENESS
Copyright ©1996 by Shirley Lamb
ISBN 0-9612364-3-4

Published by Shirley Lamb Ministries
1619 E 56th St, Tulsa, OK 74105-6932
Printed in the United States of America.

Healing for the Broken-Hearted

SLcM

In dedication to those who would be totally free of unforgiveness.

CONTENTS

ACKNOWLEDGMENT

I am deeply indebted to Jon Eargle, Bridge Building Ministries, for the truths learned and shared in this book.

My husband, Bob, and I first attended a weekend seminar by Jon in 1978. Jon taught that Jesus has provided healing for our emotional wounds even as he has for our physical wounds and infirmities.

Later, Jon and his lovely wife, Cathie, played an important role in my own journey to wholeness.

Jon taught a Pastoral Counseling Class which laid the foundation for my own counseling and prayer ministry of the past fourteen years. It was through him that I learned that Jesus is as eager to heal our past hurts and rejections as he is to heal current problems and infirmities.

Through operating in the gifts of the Holy Spirit, the Lord can get to the heart or root of any stronghold or hindrance in our lives. Then He can heal and remove the blockage so we can be that person the Lord Jesus has called us to be.

I am also deeply grateful to Bonnie Ramsey for sharing her gifting of editing and the hours she has prayerfully poured over this manuscript. Her suggestions have greatly increased the readability and understandings I am attempting to convey.

May God bless you in your journey to spiritual and emotional healing and wholeness. It all begins with learning how to forgive from your heart.

Shirley Lamb

1

DISCOVERY

The God of Peace

I remember when Jesus began the process of healing in my soul. It seemed that "all hell broke loose" as the old saying goes. Everything that had seemed normal (e.g., ease of controlling anger) began to be turned upside down and I no longer had peace of mind and heart. At times I felt like crying out, "Stop! Stop this train of life. I want to get off!"

Then one day in my Bible reading I came across the following scriptures:

This is God's will, even your **sanctification**. *(I Thessalonians 4:3)*

May the God of peace Himself **sanctify** *you through and through—that is, separate you from profane things, make you pure and wholly consecrated to God—and may your whole spirit and soul and body be preserved sound and complete and found blameless at the coming of our Lord Jesus Christ, the Messiah. (I Thessalonians 5:23 AMP)*

Sanctification is a Bible word that literally means to purify. We know what it means to use a water purifier. It takes the impurities out of the water. Did you know that we can also be purified? You might say, "You mean I don't have to live with all the 'dirt' that has been done to me?" That's right! You can be cleaned up, purified! Isn't that great news?

The phrase "separate you from profane things" caught my attention. The dictionary definition of "profane" was very interesting:

> **PROFANE**: *unholy, common or vulgar; to misuse, defile; to treat with irreverence; violate the sanctity of. The medieval Latin definition, to desecrate.*

This took me to the word "defile:"

> **DEFILE**: *to make foul or impure; tarnish, corrupt the chastity of; moral or physical pollution.*

It seems our whole society is defiled! Everywhere we turn we read or hear of situations and circumstances that have caused defilement to occur.

This is why the above verses are doubly important for us today. Without the finished work of Christ on the cross, we would be hopeless in our search to live a holy life.

But look who does the purifying—the God of peace! Could this really be true? When I asked the Lord to sanctify me I felt as though I had lost my peace!

Then He showed me the analogy of a glass of muddy water. One way to replace the water is to hold the glass under the faucet and "flush out" the dirty water with the pressure of the clean water coming from the faucet.

This is what was happening in me. When I yielded myself to this sanctification process, the Lord began "flushing out" those negative attitudes. There were times when unexplainable anger would make me want to lash out for seemingly no reason! As these feelings came to the surface, I certainly did lose my peace! He was making me **pure** and separating me from the **impurities** in my life.

Why do we have to go through all that process? Look again at I Thessalonians 5:23: So that our whole (healed, perfectly sound) spirit and whole soul and whole body can be preserved blameless at the coming of our Lord Jesus Christ.

One day as I was thinking about this a question popped into my mind. Does this mean that if our spirit and soul and body are not whole, healed, and perfectly sound, that we will not be blameless at the coming of Jesus?

Then I sensed the Lord was telling me to read on. The next verse reads

*Faithful is He who is calling you to Himself and utterly trustworthy, and He will also do it (that is, He will fulfill His call by **hallowing** and keeping you). (I Thessalonians 5:24 AMP)*

In Jesus' prayer for his disciples, he asked his Father to "*sanctify them by the truth.*" The NIV footnote defines sanctify as "set apart for sacred use or make holy." Jesus goes on to say,

Your Word is truth. As you sent me into the world, I have sent them into the world. For them I sanctify myself, that they too may be truly sanctified. (John 17:17-19 NIV)

This says to me that all we need to do is be willing and say, Yes, Lord, I give you permission to sanctify me. The rest is up to Him. He will do it.

PRAYER

Father, in Jesus Name, I give you permission to begin the work of sanctification in my soul. I confess to you my wrong reactions to negative attitudes. I ask for and believe I receive Your forgiveness. And now that I have Your forgiveness, I choose to pass it on. As an act of my will, I forgive and release those who offended me. In Jesus' Name. Amen.

2

A BIBLICAL BASIS

Let's consider our question of a few moments ago, Why do we have to go through all that process of purification? Do we have an understanding from I Thessalonians 5:24 that the God of peace will do it for us?

As I was pondering this issue, I felt to again look at verse 24 in the Amplified Bible. The parenthesis says, "He will fulfill His call by **hallowing** and keeping you."

Hallow? What does that mean? Again I pulled Strong's Concordance off the shelf! Little did I know I was in for such an exciting find! Will you join me?

*I am the Lord which **hallows** you. (Leviticus 20:8; 21:8,15,23; 22:9,32)*

Six times the priests were told this, in case they didn't get it the first time!

HALLOW: *Old Testament definition: to be clean. To make or pronounce clean (ceremonially or morally). New Testament definition: to make holy, purify, or consecrate.*

Who or what has been made holy?

15

The law and the commandments. (Romans 7:12)

The temple of God, and you are that temple (I Corinthians 3:17). Your body is the temple. (I Corinthians 6:19)

*I want men everywhere to lift up **holy** hands in prayer, without anger or disputing. (I Timothy 2:8 NIV)*

*...Build yourself up on your most **holy** faith, praying... (Jude 20 NIV)*

*You ought to live **holy** and godly lives... (II Peter 3:11 NIV)*

*God chose us in Christ before the creation of the world to be **holy** and blameless in his sight. (Ephesians 1:4 NIV)*

*You were taught to **put off** your old self, which is being corrupted by its deceitful desires; and to be made new in the attitude of your minds; and to **put on** the new self, created to be like God in true righteousness and **holiness**. Therefore... put off falsehood...Get rid of all bitterness, rage and anger, brawling and slander, along with every form of malice... **forgiving** each other, just as in Christ God forgave you. (Ephesians 2:22-25,31-32 NIV)*

*Christ loved the church and gave himself up for her to make her **holy**, cleansing her by the washing with water through the word, and to present her to himself as a radiant church, without stain or wrinkle or any other blemish, but **holy** and blameless. (Ephesians 5:25-27 NIV)*

*Once you were **alienated** from God and **were enemies in your minds** because of your evil behavior. But now He has reconciled you by Christ's physical body through death to present you **holy** in his sight, without blemish and free from accusation—if you continue in your faith, established and firm, not moved from the hope held out in the gospel. (Colossians 1:21-23 NIV)*

*...The goal of your faith..., the salvation of your souls. Concerning this salvation... **prepare your minds** for action; be self-controlled, set your hope on the grace to be given you... be **holy** in all you do; for it is written: 'Be **holy**, because I am **holy**.' Therefore, rid yourselves of all malice and all deceit, hypocrisy, envy, and slander of every kind. (I Peter 1:13-2:1 NIV)*

*...Be hospitable, one who loves what is good, who is self-controlled, upright, **holy** and disciplined. (Titus 1:8 NIV)*

*Make every effort to live in peace with all men and to be **holy; without holiness no one will see the Lord**. (Hebrews 12:14 NIV)*

Strong's primary definition for holy is:

HOLY: *sacred. (Physically pure from defilement, morally blameless, ceremonially consecrated). Ceremonially means through a system of rites or formalities, a ritual, as in the preparation of the Old Testament priests for serving at the altar (Leviticus 20-22).*

This then led me to our Lord's prayer in Matthew 6:9-12,

*Our Father in heaven, **hallowed** be your name, your kingdom come, your will be done on earth as it is in heaven...**Forgive** us our debts, as we also have forgiven our debtors...*

It seems the key to becoming holy is to continually rid ourselves of negative attitudes by forgiving. Jesus goes on to say,

*For if you **forgive** men when they sin against you, your heavenly Father will also **forgive** you. But if you do not **forgive** men their sins, your Father will not **forgive** your sins. (Matthew 6:14-15 NIV)*

*When you stand praying, if you hold anything against anyone, **forgive** him, so that your Father in heaven may **forgive** you your sins. (Mark 11:25-26 NIV)*

The apostle Paul admonishes us,

*Be kind and compassionate to one another, **forgiving** each other, just as in Christ God forgave you. (Ephesians 4:32 NIV)*

*When you were dead in your sins..., God made you alive with Christ. He **forgave** us all our sins, having canceled the written code with its regulations that was against us and that stood opposed to us; he took it away, nailing it to the cross. (Colossians 2:13-14 NIV)*

*Therefore, as God's chosen people, **holy** and dearly loved, clothe yourselves with compassion, kindness, humility, gentleness and patience. Bear with each other and **forgive** whatever grievances you may have against one another. **Forgive** as the Lord forgave you. And over all these virtues put on love, which binds them all together in perfect unity. (Colossians 3:12-14 NIV)*

These instructions are quite clear and specific regarding what it means to be holy. It is a process of putting off the negative attitudes characteristic of the "old man" and putting on the Christ-like qualities of the "new man."

It requires an act of our will to override our emotions. It involves forgiving! But what does "forgive" really mean? Again, I found an interesting definition in Strong's Concordance:

FORGIVE: *863 (from #575, a root word meaning, to send, to go): to send forth, in various applications: -cry, forgive, forsake, lay aside, leave, let alone, omit, put away, send away, remit, yield up.*

Yes, it does seem the key to becoming holy is to continually rid ourselves of negative attitudes by forgiving, sending away, yielding up, remitting the offences against us.

You may then say, "But many of the above scriptures say that all this must be done 'in Christ.' What does that mean?" I'm glad you asked that because this led to another very interesting discovery. Come along with me!

3

JESUS OUR SUBSTITUTE

Every day we read or hear news of tragedy, violence, hatred, and death. And it has been like this since the fall of man. But this is not God's will for us! God's will is that we prosper and be in health (III John 2).

The fall affected every area of man's being, spirit, soul, and body. Man's spirit was deadened in sin. His soul was burdened by sorrow, grief, heaviness, fear and despair. His body became subject to sickness, pain, infirmity and death.

Then Jesus came on the scene by being born of a woman. God the Son took on humanity and walked this earth. He came to make full provision for the salvation of our spirit, soul, and body, the three-part nature of man.

He took our sins and gave us His righteousness. He bore our sickness so we could receive His health. He became a man of sorrows in order to give us the joy of the Lord. He was despised and rejected so we could be accepted in the beloved.

A Bible word for this provision is called the atonement. In the **Old Testament**, the word **atonement** means, *to cover or cancel*. The priests were instructed to make atonement for the peoples' sins. They accomplished this by placing their hand on the head of a goat, signifying the transferring of the peoples' sins on to the goat (called a scapegoat), which was then led off into the wilderness, carrying their sins away. Jesus is the

Old Testament type of scapegoat who bore the sins of the entire human race.

In the **New Testament**, the word **atonement** means *to exchange, i.e., restore to divine favor*. Jesus died on the cross for us, taking our sins upon himself so we can identify with His death, be free from our sin, and receive of His righteousness.

Jesus took on the sin of the world by being identified with it. We take on His righteousness by being identified with it. Through the new birth we are made new creations, an heir of God and a joint heir of Christ. Our human spirit was made alive through Him.

Jesus made provision for healing for our physical bodies by being our substitute for sickness. He took our sicknesses and bore our infirmities. By His stripes we were healed. Jesus endured the whipping at Pilate's judgment hall which paid the price for our physical healing.

Jesus was also our substitute for sorrow. Isaiah says,

Surely he took up our infirmities and carried our sorrows...
He was despised and rejected by men, a man of sorrows, and
familiar with suffering. (Isaiah 53:4,3 NIV)

Jesus took the curse of rejection for us so we could be accepted. John 1:10-11 tells us

He was in the world, the world was made through Him, but
did not know Him. He came to His own and His own did not
receive Him.

That is rejection—not being received!

> **REJECTION**: *Any experience where we do not perceive that we receive the love, acceptance, affirmation or approval that we need in the way we need it, at the time that we need it, and from whom we need it. The rejection may be either real or imagined and is usually a combination of the two. It is the root cause of all emotional hurt related to people.* (Eargle, p 150)

Blood must be shed to pay for the atonement. Jesus' blood was shed on Calvary when He bore our sins on the cross. He bore our sicknesses even before He went to the cross, at the whipping post.

Christ bore our griefs and sorrows even before He stood trial. In the garden of Gethsemane he began to bear our soulish agonies when it is recorded, *My soul is exceedingly sorrowful, even unto death. (Matthew 26:38 KJV)*

Soul: Mind will emotions, memories, imaginations.

And being in an agony he prayed more earnestly: and his sweat was as it were great drops of blood falling down to the ground. (Luke 22:44 KJV)

What good is this information to us? How can we apply it and make it practical to our everyday life?

First, we can choose to believe that Jesus came to make full provision for us — spirit, soul, and body. Then, as an act of our will, we can receive the finished work of the cross in every area of our lives.

Jesus' blood avails for us only when we use it. Just like a doctor's prescription does us no good unless we use it! Every day we can "bathe" in the blood of Jesus to cleanse spirit, soul, and body from the contamination and defilement of daily living.

How are our spirits wounded? By cutting words that cause rejection. Every time we are ignored, put down, criticized unduly, it is like an arrow piercing our heart and spirit. Continued rejection will eventually cause us to reject ourselves and consider ourselves of no importance or value. Jesus' blood applied is a healing balm to our soul.

Jesus provided health and strength for our spirit, soul, and body. Let's not neglect to use what he paid such a high price to provide.

God has healing for us. The following prayer, if taken seriously, will help to restore us to wholeness. Let's pray, believing.

Father, in the name of Jesus, by faith I apply His precious blood for healing my wounded spirit and wounded heart, cleansing and healing the hurts and brokenness. I thank you that the blood washes through my mind to cleanse my conscience from dead works to serve the living God (Hebrews 9:14). I command harassing, tormenting thoughts to leave me, in the Name of Jesus! I bind my mind to the mind of Christ and my will to God's will and purpose for my life.

4

A PROSPEROUS SOUL

Then he began to teach me about III John 2: *Beloved, I wish above all things that you prosper and be in health, even as your **soul** prospers.*

What is our soul? Our soul includes the mind, will, emotions, memories, imaginations. These areas have to do with our mind or mental capacities, decisions and emotions.

This verse says that our soul must first prosper before we can prosper in physical healing and even in finances. I have noticed over the years that when I pray for healing for people's emotions, they often receive physical healing as well. Then they are free to prosper financially according to the promise of this verse!

How can my soul prosper? By being willing to forgive offenses against me and my loved ones.

Consider the scripture: *Be kind and compassionate to one another, forgiving each other, just as in Christ God forgave you. (Ephesians 4:32 NIV)*

Jesus Christ came into the world to "save" sinners (I Timothy 1:15). According to Strong's Concordance, this is the Greek word, sozo which literally means "*to deliver or protect.*" Other synonyms are "*to heal, preserve, do well, be (make) whole.*"

Most of us have been taught that to be "saved" means to be born again. There is nothing in the above definition that would limit the popular teaching to only being "born again." The term "saving of the soul" would make more sense in the broader context of healing, delivering, preserving, and making whole.

How limited is our concept of salvation when we are first born again. I guess it is much like our limited understanding of who our parents and brothers and sisters and extended family are when we are first born.

A new baby has a world of relationships to discover! It knows nothing of the character of those around it. It learns love and trust as it experiences love and faithfulness. Likewise, we have so much to learn about God and His saving grace—and the family He births us into! John 1:16 speaks of the multifaceted nature of our salvation... *from the fullness of his grace we have all received one blessing after another. (NIV)*

In 1977 when my husband and I were attending Bible School, I had an experience that caught my attention. We were learning about the functions of the ministry gifts. Our teacher was teaching that day on the work of the evangelist. As he spoke, unexplainable tears began to flow. I didn't understand why I was feeling so emotional! Upon questioning the Lord about it, He directed my gaze to the open book on my desk. The chapter title was "The Evangelist."

That day the Lord gave me the sense that He was calling me to the office of the evangelist. Believe me, I could have fainted on the spot! I had seen evangelists in action! They could raise their voices, pace back and forth on the stage, and a multitude of other activities of which I knew I was not capable!

But I determined to keep an open heart and mind. So when Bob and I went to evangelistic crusades I would sit and watch and listen, then go home devastated! "Lord, I can't do that!" would be my plea. His answer would always come back so sweetly, "I didn't ask you to do that." You see, I didn't understand that there could be more than one kind of evangelist!

In the years following the Lord began to send people to me who were broken in their spirits and hearts. He began to give me understanding on how to help them and how to pray for their healing.

Then one day a new understanding began to dawn upon me. What is the work of the evangelist? Our traditional response is that his work is the "saving of souls." Right? So what is our soul? Our mind, will, emotions, memories, imaginations.

Every Christian's soul needs to be "saved." There is so much trauma and abuse in the world today that devastates and desecrates us. We feel not only incapable, but unworthy to even think about being productive for the kingdom of God.

TRAUMA !!!

God's plan and design in creating us in His image, with a trinity of spirit, soul, and body, was so that our trinity would flow together and work together to accomplish His plans and purposes. God has made provision through the cross of Christ for us to be healed in spirit, soul, and body.

When trauma occurs, it momentarily interrupts the God-designed flow of our trinity, causing a glitch, a temporary paralysis. By it we are thrown off guard, so to speak. It causes us to feel scattered and fragmented and confused.

Webster's definition of trauma: **Pathological**: A body injury produced by violence, or a thermal or chemical agent. To traumatize is to injure tissues by force. It causes an abnormal condition to be produced. **Psychiatry**: a startling experience that has a lasting effect on mental life.

This momentary experience will have a lasting effect not only on our mental life, as Mr. Webster indicates, but also on our physical, emotional, and spiritual life, since the thing that effects one part affects all parts. Like whiplash, it may not show up for weeks, months, or years, but it **will** show up.

In this age of violence we are constantly being traumatized. This slows down our efficiency and our effectiveness, causing us to be less productive, less fruitful.

While working as a music therapist on the surgery floor at City of Faith some years ago, the Lord began to teach me how to pray concerning the trauma of surgery. My job quickly became very exciting and fulfilling as I worked with the Lord in ministering to the surgery patients. We saw many miracles and some very rapid healings!

The knowledge I gained at City of Faith has carried over into this ministry of praying for precious people who have experienced trauma. Then and now, the Lord and I help them to restore their wholeness so they can get on with their life.

PRAYER: Father, in Jesus name, I pray right now for each one reading this book. I ask you to reveal to them any area of trauma in their lives that you would like to heal by the power of your Word, your Name, and your blood. Amen.

This is the area of heaviest anointing in my ministry. I have accepted the place God has made for me. He has given me the grace to counsel and pray with those whose hearts have been broken, whose spirits have been wounded. This is the work of the evangelist, the "saving" of souls!

How do we know if our soul is prospering? Perhaps the following questions will help to delineate our answer:

1. Is our **mind** in agreement with the Word of God?

2. Is our **will** in any given situation the same as the Lord's will about that situation?

3. Are our **emotions** reflecting His emotions, or is it easy for us to "fly off the handle" when someone pushes our button?

4. Are our **memories** peaceful, or do some of them cause our stomach to be tied into knots?

5. Are we casting down **vain imaginations**, or are they running wild, going off in directions that are not in agreement with the Word of God? Any endeavor we are pursuing that is not in agreement with God's will for our life may be classified as a "vain imagination."

Our imagination is God-given. This is our avenue for pursuing the dreams that God has given us. The Bible does not say imaginations are wrong. It says we are to cast down vain imaginations and every high thing that exalts itself against the knowledge of God (II Corinthians 10:5).

How about it? Is your soul prospering? If any question was answered negatively, may your heart be blessed as you continue to read. I pray for courage and for a spirit of understanding and revelation be yours as these questions are answered, and you learn how to overcome obstacles to successful Christian living.

Allow me to share with you a poem written by my mother which expresses this concept.

A PALACE FOR THE KING

I was just a tiny, dirty shack
At the edge of a great city,
With nothing very different
From all the surrounding shacks.

But the Lord took one look at me,
And with deep compassion, moved in.

He swept the sticky cobwebs of inferiority
From the walls and ceilings of my rooms.
Vigorously he shook the dust of inadequacy
From the curtains, rugs and bedding.

He polished the greasy scum of guilt
From every window and made them crystal clear.

Far back in the dark recesses of my attic
He found stacks of old resentments and hatreds.
They had to be carried out one by one,
Carefully examined and totally destroyed.

And with meticulous care He swept
The litter of fears from every closet.

Then with tender love shining from His eyes,
He flooded every room with the fresh air of
Hope and faith and trust, and painted everything
With several coats of Christian Love.

He set every room ablaze with
The unwavering light of the Holy Spirit.

With gentleness in His hands,
He brought in immeasurable amounts
Of the luscious fruits of righteousness.
He filled all my bowls to overflowing.

He set out vases filled
With bouquets of joy and laughter.

I was a very small shack, dirty and unkempt,
Miserable, unlovely and very unlivable.
Now the Holy Spirit is buffing, polishing and cleansing.
He is making of me a palace fit for a King.

I am a dwelling place of the Most High,
A living tribute to the Lord our God!

--- Dorothy Payton Robinson
(Shirley Lamb's mother)

5

REJECTION

It wasn't until the winter of 1978 that I began to realize the truth of some things that I didn't know were possible. I knew that Jesus died on the cross for our sins in order for us to be born again and obtain eternal life. I knew that Jesus took the stripes on His back so our physical bodies might be healed of our sicknesses.

But I didn't know that He also died on the cross for healing for our soul. In my studies, I learned that our soul is the mental and emotional part of us, i.e., our mind, will, emotions, imaginations, and memories.

It seems like a lot of us get messed up in our minds these days. And there are a lot of damaged emotions with all the violence going on—the drug abuse, incest, divorce, and the dehumanization of our society.

I know that God is a loving heavenly father who doesn't want us to hurt any more than a good earthly father would want his children to hurt. But why are so many of us "hurting" these days?

I believe the number one cause of emotional hurts is related to rejection. Therefore, recognizing rejection is a key to emotional healing.

That winter of 1978 I began to learn about "rejection." It was then that I heard a definition for rejection that made a lot of sense to me. For the first time I could identify a "hurt" on the inside of me.

For many years I experienced a pain, like a hurt in my heart. Sometimes it was as a dull ache, sometimes more acute. I didn't know I could be without this pain, but assumed it was just a natural part of life.

Then one day Bob and I attended a seminar where we heard a definition for rejection that caused me to sit up and take notice. This definition has been a key term in my healing, in becoming whole in my soul. It turned on a light for me. It gave me understanding. Because, for the first time, I realized that "rejection" was the name of the hurt I had been feeling. Remember our definition of rejection:

REJECTION: *Any experience where we do not perceive that we receive the love, acceptance, affirmation or approval that we need in the way we need it, at the time that we need it, and from whom we need it. The rejection may be either real or imagined and is usually a combination of the two. It is the root cause of all emotional hurt related to people. (Eargle, p 150)*

What happens when we receive rejection? We get resentful, possibly angry or bitter. It causes us to feel unimportant or insignificant. It causes us to put up walls so we won't get rejected again. This is the Number One reason we put up walls that we carry with us all our lives. This is why we get messed up in our minds. This is the wounding that sometimes goes so deep it is difficult to put names on it.

Hurts and slights cause negative emotions inside us. It may mean we get the wrong kind of attention, perhaps a violation. For example, let's say we experienced a robbery. The first part of us to respond will be our soul in the emotional realm of perhaps anger, fear, and eventually bitterness. In time this will lead to physical symptoms such as arthritis or any number of painful symptoms.

It seems the church focus is on the experience and the emotional response. Their solution is to ignore it by advising "It's under the blood. Don't think about it and it will go away." Whereas the world focus is on the physical symptoms resulting from the experience. Their solution is to take a pill to get rid of the pain. In both cases the cause of the pain is totally ignored.

Out of our experiences of hurt and trauma we make judgments. These judgments are made because we have been violated. This means someone entered my "space" without permission. So I make a decision against being vulnerable in the future. I make a decision to be more in control.

Because these judgments are made out of hurt and anger which lead to bitterness, we call these "bitter root judgments" (Sandford, see Chapter 14). They start with a violation (emotional, mental, or physical) that was caused by trauma.

What may be trauma for one may not be trauma for another. It depends upon whether we were vulnerable in that area.

Dr. Charles Stanley, in a message entitled, "Forgiving Hurts We Don't Deserve" has stated

"The poison of an unforgiving spirit damages the entire person. Someone with an angry or bitter heart is trapped in his own bitterness, unable to give and receive love freely. Feelings are frozen. And this bondage eventually harms others. The tension, anxiety, and guilt mounting on the inside are often expressed by sudden outbursts of frustration or criticism of family and friends."

Our memories are frozen frames of time. Bitter root judgments put a person in a time capsule, freezing them in time. The emotional reality of current hurts is triggered by trauma of the past.

This is why adults act childish in certain areas of their life. They experienced a trauma which caused a block in their emotional development from that age.

Hurt and trauma often cause us to feel rejected. Do you have an empty place or a hurt in your heart like I did, and you don't know why? Does that hurt cause you to get angry or resentful when there seems to be no outward reason?

Do you have voids in your life that cause you to seek friendships in the wrong places or from the wrong people? Try calling those voids "rejection" and see if it brings light to the dark places.

PRAYER

I invite you to pray the following prayer with me as a first step in the healing process:

Dear Lord Jesus, I recognize I need a savior and healer. Come into my heart and fill the ache I now recognize as rejection. Fill these holes with your healing love. I ask you to turn my sorrow into joy. Set my captive heart free to be all you've planned for me to be. Thank you for that seed you've planted in my heart this day. In Jesus' name, Amen.

6

REAL OR IMAGINED

Let's look at it further. Rejection may be real, or it may be imagined. Most of the rejection I was experiencing was imagined. What I perceived as rejection in reality may not have been the case. However, as far as our emotions are concerned, the feelings are real. Sometimes our interpretations of the facts are in error.

When I was young, my mother used to tell me that I wore my heart on my sleeve. I didn't really know what she meant. You know, I couldn't **see** it out there. It meant that my feelings were showing. I was feeling rejected often.

There is a difference between actual and perceived rejection. For example, as a youngster, piano lessons were important from age eight. Every spring there would be a recital so we could "show off" the progress we had made that year for our parents.

It was hard work memorizing those classical pieces. At recital time my mother was always there, but my dad never came. I was always disappointed because I wanted and needed his support and approval. But he always had something more important to do. This is an example of real rejection.

Perceived rejection is imagining others are rejecting us, causing us to feel rejected, though we have no proof it is so.

An example might be when some classmates are standing in a circle talking, then glance your way and go back to talking and laughing among themselves. You just KNOW they are talking about you!

This causes you to feel rejected, though it was not intended. But because this was your perception of the situation, you felt rejected. And as far as our emotions are concerned, our feelings are real and need to be acknowledged through confession and forgiveness.

Yes, our feelings of rejection may be mostly imaginary. For a humorous example, did you hear about the man who was so super sensitive that he had to stop going to football games? You see, every time the team got into a huddle, he thought they were talking about him! (Seamands, p 18)

How much better for our hearts to be securely nestled in His loving hands, rather than dangling out there on the end of our sleeve, vulnerable to every "wind of criticism or rejection." If our heart is hidden in Christ, then everything that comes to us is filtered through His absolute, unfailing love for us. His love then becomes that healing balm that instantly covers the wounds rejection brings.

We know the Word of God is the ultimate truth. But there has to be a stronghold in our thought processes from some real rejections for the imaginations to even have a foothold. The rejection we receive is usually a combination of both the real and the imagined. It is the root cause of emotional hurts.

7

SIGNIFICANT PEOPLE

R ejections are based on a real and significant past rejection from a primary person in our life (Seamands, p 18).

Our parents are the most significant primary people in our lives. However, others who are very close might be brothers or sisters, aunts and uncles, cousins, grandparents, or even teachers. Primary people in our lives are those who have authority over us and significantly shape and influence our lives.

Often those rejections are so devastating and painful that at the time they happen we pretend they aren't there. We attempt to have amnesia concerning that painful event. This allows us the privilege of denying that the rejection really happened (Eargle, p 7).

Repeated rejections from significant people in our lives gradually build until we are "feeling" rejected all the time.

For example, sometimes well-meaning parents point out the faults and shortcomings of their children to challenge them to do their best. Unless this is offset with compliments and encouragement, children may grow up thinking they can never do anything "good enough." This then transfers to their perception of how God feels about them, causing them to think they can never be good enough for God to care about them.

When rejection becomes a stronghold, even an innocent sleight may cause us to feel rejected, like when someone doesn't smile at us when we think they should. And that causes us to believe they don't like us. It may cause us to feel fearful and timid, assessing another's worth as far greater than our own.

Hurts and trauma from significant people cause negative attitudes and reactions inside us and often cause us to feel rejected. Not dealing with the rejection causes emotions and attitudes to develop within us that cause us to walk in sin. Our sin is our repressed emotions of anger, resentment, jealousy.

I have learned that repeated rejection may lead to resentment. This may lead to anger and bitterness. If the downward spiral is unchecked it may then lead to hatred. The Bible tells us if we have hate in our heart toward someone, it is akin to murder.

For example, what happens when we receive rejection? We get resentful, possibly angry. It causes us to feel unimportant or insignificant. It causes us to put up walls, so we won't get rejected again.

Fear of rejection causes us to believe that what we have to say doesn't really matter because it is not important anyway. It causes us to put ourselves down if it happens often enough. This is self-rejection which leads to a low self-image (Eargle, p 20). Because of all these reasons, the Lord revealed to me that taking on rejection keeps us from being whole.

Sin keeps us from the very best God has to offer. If we could see that sin keeps us from the very best God has to offer, we would want to know where there was sin in our lives. Because sin separates us from God and separates us from His promises.

Circumstances have tricked us into believing a lie from the enemy in order to keep us in an area of sin. This can then bring us into bondage. Romans 8:15 is God's antidote to bondage. *"We have not received a spirit of bondage again to fear, but we have received a spirit of adoption, whereby we can cry Abba, Father."*

God wants to set us free into the area of liberty! In the midst of trials, conflict, and infirmity, God wants us to have a peace that passes all understanding. He wants us to have a joy and to be a light in the darkness so we can radiate Jesus.

The Psalmist wrote, *Who may ascend into the hill of the Lord? And who may stand in His holy place? He who has clean hands and a pure heart, who has not lifted up his soul to falsehood, and has not sworn deceitfully. (Psalms 24:3-4)*

One writer says,

...we cannot even find the hill of the Lord, much less ascend it, if there is deceit in our soul. How does one serve in God's holy place if his heart is unclean? It is only the pure in heart who perceive God.

It is this upward call of God which we pursue (Philippians 3:14). Yet the soul within us is hidden, crouching in fears and darkness, living in a world of untruths and illusions. This is our inner man, the soul God seeks to save. We seek holiness, but true holiness arises from this hidden place of our hearts.

As members of the human race, we are shrouded in ignorance. Barely do we know our world around us; even less do we know our hearts. Can we, with King David, pray *Search me, O God, and know my heart; try me and know my anxious thoughts; and see if there be any hurtful way in me, and lead me in the everlasting way. (Psalms 139:23-24)*

Concerning man's nature, we are told that, *The heart is more deceitful than all else, and is desperately sick. Who can understand it? (Jeremiah 17:9)* Quoting David again, a similar cry is heard, *Who can discern his errors? Acquit me of hidden faults. Also keep thy servant from presumptuous sins; let them not rule over me; then I shall be blameless, and I shall be acquitted of great transgression. (Psalms 19:12-13)*

There may be errors inside us that are actually ruling us without our awareness. Do we realize, for instance, how many of our actions are manipulated purely by vanity and the desire to be accepted by others? Are we aware of the fears and apprehensions that unconsciously influence so many of our decisions? We may have serious problems inside, yet still be either too proud or too insecure to admit we need help.

Our fallen thinking processes automatically justify our actions and rationalize our thoughts. Without the Holy Spirit, we are nearly defenseless against our own innate tendencies toward self-deception (Frangipane p 6-7).

No condemnation or punishment awaits our honesty of heart. We have only to repent and confess our sins to have them forgiven and cleansed. We need merely to love and embrace the truth to be delivered from sin and self-deception (Frangipane, p 8).

8

EXPOSING SIN

When we talk about sin or expose sin and the lies of the devil, it is because God has something far greater for us today. So let's open our hearts to hear. I pray right now that we receive God's spirit of wisdom, understanding, and revelation, that the eyes of our understanding be opened so we can know and understand the hope He has for us.

A definition for sin might be the following:

Sin is either a positive act in which a known divine law is violated, or a voluntary neglect to obey a positive divine command or rule or duty implied in such a command. (Legamaro, p2)

Sin can result from either transgression (rebellion) or neglect. It is contrary to God's commands. It is called lawlessness.

"Anyone who commits sin is guilty of lawlessness (breaking God's laws by transgression or neglect)... *No one who abides in Him deliberately, knowingly, habitually commits sin."* (I John 3:4-6 AMP)

Sin often begins as an attitude that is then turned into an action. Our attitude is our choice. For example, the act of entertaining evil thoughts, left unchecked, will turn into evil words, desires, and purposes.

"...everything that does not come from faith is sin." (Romans 14:23c NIV)

"Anyone, then, who knows the good he ought to do and doesn't do it, sins." (James 4:17 NIV)

Attitudes, emotions, and reactions resulting from past hurts and rejections are possibly sin that we are not recognizing. They are separating us from the promises of God and they dull our relationship with Him.

The Bible also tells us our flesh (our carnal nature) wars against our spiritual nature. (A note of clarification concerning the word "flesh": It is **not** synonymous with "body." Our body is the temple of the Holy Spirit and is to be valued and appreciated.) When we do the opposite of what our flesh says or wants, that's where the power of the Holy Spirit becomes available to us.

The power of God is far greater than the power of sin. The Holy Spirit can cancel out the power of darkness. It is through the power of the Holy Spirit that we turn around what the flesh, the world, and the devil wants for our life. Yes, our flesh (our carnal nature) will have to die, but also sickness will leave our body. Stress, confusion, and depression will leave our mind. The revelation of Jesus that we need most will come! (Legamaro, p 2)

Having said all this, let's proceed by looking at some possible reasons why hurts and rejections are separating us from the promises of God.

We can liken our hurts to a tree with roots and fruit. Those attitudes, emotions, and reactions that are manifesting in our life today, the circumstances that are being controlled by these emotions today, are just the fruit on the tree. It may manifest as an anger problem, or a drug or alcohol dependency. Often people come for prayer counseling because of the negative fruit that is manifesting in their lives and they want something done about it.

The Lord instructed me early in the ministry not to go around picking rotten fruit! It gets too messy! He said, "Go for the roots. Ask me to show you the initial circumstances that caused the 'tree' to grow to the stage we see today."

What were the circumstances that allowed the tree to take root, which caused those negative emotions to "get their foot in the door," so to speak?

Most often it goes back to early childhood. Sometimes it even goes back to pre-birth circumstances. The Lord has taught me from the scriptures regarding the child in the womb and how aware he is of his world. He is very capable of perceiving rejections and negative attitudes toward his presence there in the womb.

This is where my rejection began. It seemed to be a funny little incident my mother and I laughed about as I was growing up—the fact that before I was born I was named after my two grandfathers. I was supposed to have been James Frederick! What a surprise when I was born!

I didn't understand the significance of this until the Lord began to move me into this ministry of healing for our soul. Then I became aware that this was a very big rejection factor in my life.

I knew before I was born that I was not the "right" sex. Therefore I could not be pleasing, especially to my father who wanted a boy to help him on the farm. So, guess what he had! A tomboy. I worked very hard to fulfill the role of that boy that he needed, much preferring to work with him out in the field driving the tractor, or milking the cows, than to help mother with the housework.

You see, we work hard to fulfill our parents expectations. Then when we grow up, fall in love, get married, we work very hard to fulfill our mates expectations. If our experiences with our parents were unpleasant, we may even vow that we will never marry a person like our father or mother, but often this is exactly what we do.

So, our attitude toward our circumstances plays a large role in dealing with the rejections of our life.

9

OUR ATTITUDE TOWARD CIRCUMSTANCES

What do we do with our circumstances? Do we respond to them, or do we react to them? When we *respond* to our circumstances, it means we are not more upset than the situation warrants. We can deal with that situation properly (Eargle, p 151). In other words, we have control of our emotions when we respond to a situation.

Did you know we can be angry and not sin? According to Ephesians 4:26, "Be angry and sin not," we can respond in anger because it is appropriate. There is a right use of anger. Anger in itself is not a sinful emotion (Seamands, p 106).

I didn't always think this was so. I thought good little Christian girls didn't get angry. This caused me to deny angry and hurt feelings, pushing them down inside, and putting the lid on tight. But ignoring them didn't make them go away.

Dr. Charles Stanley has said that "hurt turns into bitterness and unforgiveness when it isn't dealt with properly. You can't ignore it and hope it will just go away. The saying that 'time heals old wounds' really isn't true; in fact, time actually causes old wounds to become infected and spread to healthy emotional tissue."

When I found that both Ephesians and the Psalms say, "*Be angry and sin not*," I thought, "Lord, this is double talk. What does it mean?"

It means we are not more upset than the situation calls for, and we are in control of our emotions. They are not controlling us.

Scripture also says, "*Don't let the sun go down on your wrath.*" (Ephesians 4:26) Deal with it that day. Don't stuff it down inside and put the lid on it. Thus, I found out it was all right to be angry in certain circumstances and this anger was not a sinful reaction.

Now, **reaction** is just the opposite of responding. To react means that we are more upset than the situation justifies, and we have much more difficulty dealing with it. In fact, our emotions are probably out of control. Usually we end up repressing or burying our feelings (Eargle, p 150).

One day I was driving our youngest son to school. He had done something that morning that really irritated me. I don't even remember what it was, but I do remember that I was very upset with him. And I was certainly venting my feelings, letting him know that I was upset.

On the way to school I was still letting him know how upset I was about what he had done. He was just sitting there very quietly, not saying anything.

Finally he turned to me and said, "You know, Mom, you are more upset about what I did than you really should be." I gulped. Then it was my turn to get very quiet. Inside myself I said, "Lord, is that right?"

I've learned that if we are more upset than the situation warrants, it is likened to someone putting his finger in an open wound. We react.

Something he said had triggered an old wound in me that was still open and festering. It caused me to lash out at him.

It wasn't what he said that was the real cause of my anger. It was because of a significant rejection that had been left unhealed inside of me. So I said, "Lord, show me what caused me to react to my son like that, to get his whole day started wrong."

And He did! I then asked the Lord to heal that wound. I confessed my own hurt and rejection resulting from a situation with my mother when I was a young teenager. I asked the Lord's forgiveness for my wrong reactions. Then I turned to my son and said, "You are absolutely right, Jim. I am sorry. Please forgive me."

He said, "No problem." You see, he already knew it was my problem and not his. Therefore, he knew to refuse to receive it as his own.

And this is another key. When someone is upset with us it may not be our problem. So we shouldn't automatically assume that he is angry with us because of something we did, assuming that we are the cause of his anger. There may be several reasons why it is his problem and not ours. Most probably he was already angry before we came on the scene.

I have learned it is not our circumstances that control us, but it is our *reaction* to our circumstances, our attitude toward them that control us (Eargle, p 20-22). If Jim had taken on my anger and if he had reacted in anger toward me, then his circumstances would have been controlling him.

51

However, since he is a wise son, he didn't allow that to happen. He knew the problem was not his, so he did not react to my anger. Thus, it is not our circumstances that control us. It is our *reaction* to those circumstances that control us. Do you see the difference?

We admire people who don't let their circumstances control them—who come out with a good attitude. They find something good to say about their circumstances, however adverse they may seem to us. This is according to Scripture, because Romans 8:28 says, *"All things work together for our good if we love God and are called according to His purpose."* But how many of us can do that? Isn't it more fun to gripe and complain and have a pity party? The problem with a pity party is that nobody comes but you, and that makes for a lonesome party!

You may say, then, what do we do with the feelings of anger? What do we do when we feel rejected? What do we do when we feel afraid, when fear paralyzes us? What do we do when we "fly off the handle?" I'm glad you asked that! There is a solution for healing of the hurts and rejections in our lives.

I have learned five important steps which have been invaluable aids to the HOW of forgiving. They are:

1. RECOGNIZE our wrong reactions which are keeping us from the very best God has for us and acknowledging them as sin.

2. CONFESS our sin by verbalizing the feelings we have as a result of what was done to us; how it caused us to feel.

3. RECEIVE God's forgiveness for ourselves.

4. FORGIVE and release those who have hurt us.

5. RELEASE the hurt, resentment, and rejection.

"That's easy!" you may say. I know these steps sound so simple. But they were given by the Spirit of God and it is not an easy matter to grasp them with our mind. So let's start at the beginning of these steps to healing the hurts inside.

These five steps are also listed at the back of the book for a quick and easy guide in praying through a difficult situation.

10

HOW TO RECOGNIZE OUR HURT

If we confess our sins, He is faithful and just to forgive our sins and to cleanse us from all unrighteousness. (I John 1:9)

Recognizing our wrong reactions that keep us in bondage to the law of sin and death is the first step to forgiving others.

The writer of the Hebrews encourages us to *"throw off everything that hinders and the sin that so easily entangles, and let us run with perseverance the race marked out for us." (Hebrews 12:1b NIV)* A friend was pondering this verse, wondering what was the difference between hindrances and sins, when she sensed the Lord speaking to her heart. "Hindrance is what is done to you, but sin is what you do."

Notice the first word,"If." "**If** we confess our sins" -- it is conditional. Yes, we have a part to play. If we confess. If we don't confess, we don't get forgiven, do we? God's grace cannot cover what we won't own (admit to).

As parents, if our child came to us admitting a wrong-doing, our disciplinary action would probably tend to be more lenient. But what if we learned of his wrongdoing from another source, then confronted him only to have him deny or lie about wrong doing? Would there be the same grace available to him?

If we confess **our** sins...

The first step to forgiving others is to recognize our sins resulting from the hurts and rejections we received. That is, we must recognize that we have indeed missed the mark of God's standard. Missing the mark is our sin, our shortcoming, *even if we are the innocent victim!*

Recognizing our wrong reactions as sin is the first step to forgiving others. We may have been just standing there minding our own business, when suddenly we were violated or attacked! We can either respond or react to such attacks. If we react, we risk falling into sin. Our sin may be that we become angry. Or fearful. Or resentful. Feeling "put upon." Perhaps feeling isolated and lonely. Or rejected.

Our reactions, yes, our negative emotions, probably are very justified. So why are they wrong? Because they cause us to hurt others. Often these "others" are those we love the most. For instance, recall my reaction to my son's minor error.

Any negative emotions in our life which block our journey toward wholeness may be called sins. We need to allow the Holy Spirit to convict our hearts of these sins. God is faithful. He will speak to us when we allow negative emotions to cause us to react wrongly to these surprise attacks.

Our wrong reactions not only hurt others; they hurt us and distort our perspective. How? Because they cause us to make judgments based on our hurts rather than on the truth of the Word of God. Making judgments based on our hurts is like setting the course of our lives on the tracks of those judgments that have been laid out before us. Later in life we may have a change of heart and want to change the direction of our life. But it can only change if the negative judgment is repented of and renounced, recognizing the cross as the stopping place for our sin. (Sandford, chapter 14)

Negative emotions will even distort our perspective of God. Allowing negative emotions to dominate our lives blinds us to the fact that God loves us and does not want us to hurt. In other words, our sin is the wrong reactions we have toward those who have hurt us.

For example, how is a small child "sinning" by feeling rejected by a parent, sibling, peer, etc.? If habitual rejection of a child is followed by the forced response of stuffing or burying his emotions, then an unnatural pattern is created for life. The child is not whole, not normal. Again, let me stress that *he may be an innocent victim.*

Even innocent victims respond to their circumstances. What about the fact that you learn to hate, or resent, or to escape into an unreal world? (Seamands, p 21)

When we react wrongly to an attack we are punishing ourselves for what someone else did to us, even years ago. A very graphic current example is from the popular Disney film, The Lion King. He believed the lie his uncle whispered into his ear. His reaction to a false accusation is a graphic example of what happens when we carry false guilt—not only what happens to us, but also to others because we have abrogated our authority!

These reactions are not wrong because they are not justified, but because they are wrong for us. Wrong because they hurt us and distort our perspective. Wrong because God loves us and does not want us to hurt.

They are wrong because they cause us to hurt others, especially those we love most. Wrong because many times we are punishing ourselves for what someone else did to us, even years ago.

It makes no sense to punish ourselves in this manner. Doing so is not good for anybody -- us or the one who offended us. It is self-defeating and self-destructive! (Eargle, p 37)

We are responsible for our actions. We will never receive healing for our damaged emotions until we stop blaming everyone else and accept our responsibility (Seamands, p 21).

11

HOW TO CONFESS OUR HURT

The second step is to begin to confess any hurt, including feeling rejected.

(Remember our definition of rejection: *Not receiving the love, affirmation, or attention we need at the time we need it, in the way we need it, from the one we need it.*)

Would you believe I initially found myself confessing feelings of rejection 10, 20, 30 times a day? It seemed that every time I turned around I was having to confess, "Lord, I did it again. I felt rejected again. In Jesus' name I ask You to forgive me."

Sometimes I was not conscious that I was feeling rejected, but then that pain in my heart would intensify and I would think, "Hmm. There it is again."

This caused me to stop and evaluate what had just happened. Had I felt rejected just now? And sure enough, I had. It had been such a normal, natural feeling that I had just overlooked it. Some things we think we just have to live with!

The Lord would not let me overlook anything. He wanted it dealt with, recognized, and confessed. Because when it was dealt with, the hurts and rejections that were causing the blockage to emotional maturity could be healed. Then the enemy would have no more place to get a foothold in my life.

Nevertheless, the pain would come back again, and I would have to evaluate it. And sure enough, I would have to confess again, "Lord, I did it again. I felt rejected just now, and I ask Your forgiveness, in Jesus' name."

I got so tired of confessing my feelings of rejection that it was making me angry, causing me to confess through clench-ed teeth. Even doing that was all right, because the Lord knew my heart. He knew that I wanted to be clean and pure before Him.

To **CONFESS** *means to acknowledge, to own or admit as true, therefore to agree with God, that what He is saying to us is right.*

To confess automatically includes renouncing sin and repent-ing (turning around) because we stop making alibis and blaming others. We line up with what God is saying on the subject (Adams, p 120). This allows us to experience God's forgiveness.

Let's look at I John 1:9 again: *"If we confess our sins..."* Remember, the sins we are zeroing in on are our wrong reactions when others wound or reject us in some way, or when we think they have.

If we confess whose sin? Our sins, our wrong reactions. We Christians are experts in confessing the other person's sin!

"Lord, look what they did -- thus and thus and thus, but I forgive them, in Jesus' name!"

Whose sin are we confessing? Theirs! But my Bible says, *"If we confess **our** sins."*

What if it wasn't our fault? What if we were the helpless victim?

Did we feel rejected by what they did? Did it make us feel angry? Belittled? Left out? Isolated? Violated?

I call these feelings "sin." Why? Because they churn on the inside of us and that causes us to lose our peace.

Most of us would protest, "These are perfectly understandable reactions!" But God says, "They are sin!"

Why? Because they hinder our ability to forgive those who have sinned against us. So the fruit of these feelings is unforgiveness. And God calls unforgiveness sin.

Doesn't He understand why we feel the way we do? Absolutely yes, but His response is, "How you feel is understandable, but it is not acceptable."

We must deal with the sin of unforgiveness in the same way that we deal with any other sin. "If we confess **our** sins He is faithful and just to forgive us and to cleanse us from all unrighteousness."

The Amplified Bible renders I John 1:9 this way:

If we freely admit that we have sinned and confess our sins, He is faithful and just (true to His own nature and promises) and will forgive our sins (dismiss our lawlessness) and continuously cleanse us from all unrighteousness -- everything not in conformity to His will in purpose, thought and action.

Unforgiveness is not in conformity to God's will. The beautiful thing is that when we are set free from unforgiveness, we can also be set free from the angry feelings we have had toward those who have sinned against us.

King David knew the secret! In Psalm 32 he announces

Blessed is he whose transgressions are forgiven, whose sins are covered.

Blessed is the man whose sin the Lord does not count against him and in whose spirit is no deceit.

When I kept silent, my bones wasted away through my groaning all day long. For day and night your hand was heavy upon me; my strength was sapped as in the heat of summer. Selah

Then I acknowledged my sin to you and did not cover up my iniquity. I said, "I will confess my transgressions to the Lord" (AMP: continually unfolding the past until all is told)—and you forgave the guilt of my sin. Selah

Therefore let everyone who is godly pray to you while you may be found; surely when the mighty waters rise, they will not reach him.

You are my hiding place; you will protect me from trouble and surround me with songs of deliverance. Selah (Psalms 32:1-7 NIV)

Notice that he doesn't say we are to go back and dig up our past. That's not our job. We give the God of Peace permission to sanctify us, to clean us up. We give Him permission to bring up those circumstances of our lives that are blocking and hindering us from moving on into that walk He has for us. Then we can move freely into His high calling.

Often times when we are violated in one way or another we feel like "Well, it's over with. Life is finished. I can't go on. I can never fulfill God's call on my life."

Frankly, I believe this is why there are so many teenage suicides today. They have been violated and they feel like life is finished and they can never be the clean vessel God can use. Oh, how they need the good news that Jesus' blood still avails. Jesus' blood can cleanse them from everything that was done to them, can heal every circumstance and violation of their life.

Again I say, we don't go digging up stuff. That's not our job. But we say, "Holy Spirit, whatever it is that is blocking me from being the person that you put me on this earth to be, then show me. Bring it up so I can deal with it."

I have a friend in Kansas in a similar ministry. Her favorite saying is "The revealing is the healing, when it is brought to the cross." Because once we know what it is, it is easy to deal with it. We are 90% home free when we know what we are dealing with because God has the answer and the solution. It is right here in His Word.

Psalm 90:8 (AMP) tells us, *"our iniquities, our secret heart and its sins, You have set in the revealing light of Your countenance."*

So, the first thing we do is to recognize our sins. Then we confess our wrong reactions we have had toward those who have hurt us; the attitudes that have developed in us since the initial hurt.

To confess means to agree with God, that what He is saying is right. Then once we confess those attitudes, the next very important step is that we receive God's forgiveness for ourselves.

12

HOW TO RECEIVE GOD'S FORGIVENESS

Now for the third step in coming into successful Christian living. After recognizing our wrong reactions as sin and confessing them to God, we need to receive His forgiveness and cleansing for ourselves.

Our understanding of God's forgiveness is greatly influenced by man's version of forgiveness. What an inaccurate measure of God's style of forgiveness!

How important it is to know that you are forgiven! Until you experience God's divine, cleansing forgiveness you cannot truly forgive those who wound you. You can't give what you don't have.

Oh, how often someone will say, "I am sorry" to us. Then we glibly respond with, "Oh, that's all right. I forgive you."

Yet all the while we are thinking, "And you better not do it again!" Or, we have difficulty looking that person in the eyes the next time we see him. And we go away as angry as we were before they said, "I'm sorry." And as angry as we were before we said, "I forgive you."

Tell me, did we really forgive them? NO. We said the words off the top of our head, but they didn't come out of our heart.

How do I know? Because of the lack of peace in our heart. The Bible says we are to forgive "from our heart." Unless we do, we will be eaten up inside with the bad feelings. If these feelings are left unchecked, they will manifest in physical symptoms.

A friend of mine attended a family reunion. At this reunion was a woman who had traveled a great distance to attend. As my friend was visiting with her, the woman began to tell of a devastating experience in her life.

As she spoke, her face flushed with anger toward those responsible. It was as though it were a fresh and current experience in her life. When asked when this incident happened, the woman replied, "Twenty years ago this month."

She was then asked if these people knew they had offended her. Her reply was "No, and I'm not about to tell them, either!"

Who was being eaten up on the inside, the woman or the offenders?

Why can't we just say "I forgive you" and everything be okay? The reason is we haven't forgiven from our hearts.

When we haven't forgiven from our hearts, we have no forgiveness to give to others. We are still bound by our sin, by our wrong reactions to the sins committed against us. And they are still bound by our anger, resentment, and unforgiveness. We must have forgiveness for ourselves in any given situation before we will have it to give.

I cannot give you a gift of something unless I already have received it for myself. I cannot give you a $100 bill, for example, unless I already have it in my possession. Once it is mine, then I am free to give it. Neither can we give the gift of forgiveness until we have it in our possession. And it is not in our possession until we forgive from our heart.

We know Christ came to pay the price for our sin, pardoning us. But have we actually received that pardon for every area of our lives?

If we have areas of hurt in our lives -- physically, emotionally, spiritually -- then we have not yet received Christ's complete redemption. We must recognize these areas, confess them as sin, and receive His forgiveness. His grace cannot cover what we won't own up to, or admit.

God wants us to be very specific in our confessing and receiving of forgiveness. When a surgeon operates, we want him to be very specific, only removing the infected area. "General surgery" won't do!

If are we going to appropriate this truth for ourselves in the emotional area, we must get very specific in confessing our wrong reactions. A general statement like, "I'm angry, Lord. Please forgive me," doesn't allow Him to touch your heart and set you free of anger.

Open your heart before Him. Say, "This is why I am angry! This is why I feel rejected!" Then name specific occasions and the persons involved.

As you do, Jesus will prune away your anger and heal the hurt your wounds have brought. He will forgive you, and having received His forgiveness, you can forgive the one who wounded you.

We might pray like this, indicating the specific situation we are struggling with:

*Father, in the name of Jesus, I confess to you that I felt rejected, angry, and resentful in that particular situation. I felt left out, degraded, put upon by (name the individuals). And I confess it to you as sin. I receive your forgiveness according to I John 1:9 which says, "If we confess **our** sins, you are faithful and just to forgive us and to cleanse us from all unrighteousness."*

When we do, we are forgiven the moment we ask. We don't have to wait 10 minutes or 24 hours or do penance before He will pass His forgiveness on to us.

He will forgive you. Is this mind-boggling to you? Yes, He will forgive you in order to be true to His Word. Jesus told Peter to forgive seventy times seven (Matthew 18:22; Luke 17: 3-4). If humans are to do that, how much greater is God's ability and how much more gracious is He to forgive us.

If we confess, He is faithful and just to forgive. That's that! As soon as the words have left our lips!

We just have to say, "I am sorry, Father, and I receive Your forgiveness." His forgiveness is not based on our feeling or on our righteousness. Forgiveness is based on the fact that Jesus shed his blood and paid the price. 2 Corinthians 5:20-21 says to us, *"Be reconciled to God. God made him who had no sin to be sin for us, so that in him we might become the righteousness of God." (NIV)*

Not to receive God's forgiveness for ourselves would despise the act of Jesus shedding His blood for our forgiveness of sins.

This brings up another challenge. "Why should God forgive me? I've done this before, and I know I'll do it again down the line, given the right circumstances. I can't help it. So why should God forgive me? Besides that, I don't feel worthy to receive His forgiveness."

There are those with whom I have prayed, amazingly strong Christians, some of whom were already in the ministry. I thought this would be an easy step for them. But it has been incredibly difficult because even they did not feel worthy to receive!

I am laboring over this step with you because it is so important. And it sounds so e-a-s-y, but just try it!

Many of us have difficulty in receiving God's forgiveness for ourselves because of our lack of self-worth. We say, "Besides, I don't feel worthy to receive His forgiveness."

But our forgiveness isn't dependent upon our worth. Our forgiveness is a gift of His inconceivable grace. He has commanded us to forgive—even ourselves!

We forgive out of obedience to the Word of God. He has already determined in His heart to forgive us. He already paid the price with the precious blood of Jesus that was shed for the forgiveness of our sins. When we recognize our sin and confess it to Him, He forgives us.

Why isn't it easy? Because it is a spiritual matter, not just a mental exercise.

When I first began this important exercise, I had a piece of paper with all this written out. I had to carefully follow through the above forgiveness prayer word by word with my finger. Though at first I tried, I just could not say it off the top of my head.

There is a pain when we allow a doctor to remove a diseased portion of our body. Likewise there is pain when we allow God to remove a diseased portion of our spirit or our soul. And that is what we are doing when we open our hearts to Him and confess our sins. He removes that diseased portion of our spirit and pours out His healing grace. Then our healing begins with His blood cleansing and disinfecting the wound.

We must first receive it for ourselves in order to have it to pass on to those who have offended us. Remember, I can't give something away unless I already have it in my possession. For example, I can't give my bible to someone until someone else first gives it to me and I have it in my possession. But once I have it in my possession I am free to give it away, if I want. It is the same way with forgiveness.

Having received His healing, cleansing, forgiveness, we are free to pass it on, to forgive others.

Always remember, if we confess our sins, He is faithful and just to forgive us. Then we must receive His forgiveness. What a precious gift His forgiveness is!

13

HOW TO BE OBEDIENT TO FORGIVE

First, we recognize our sin. Second, we confess our wrong reactions. Third, we receive God's forgiveness for ourselves. Then the fourth step is to forgive. We need to pass on the forgiveness we have received for ourselves, pass it on to the one who has offended us.

Dr. Ed Cole speaks of the principle of release (Cole, p 126). He explains that we retain, keep, or hang on to what we do not let go of or release. For example, in John 20:23, Jesus states:

If you forgive anyone his sins, they are forgiven (released), and if you do not forgive, they are not forgiven (released).

You retain what you do not release. This is one way sins are passed down from generation to generation.

In II Corinthians 2:10-11, we are admonished to forgive so that Satan not get the advantage over us. *We forgive not necessarily because we feel like it, but because it is right for both us and others.*

It is an act of the will, not an emotional feeling. Unwillingness to forgive will short-circuit the entire healing process. This also includes forgiving ourselves.

Early in my prayer counseling "career," a young woman temporarily moved to Tulsa from the east coast for counseling. Her life was filled with trauma and devastation. She had been very suicidal, but heard about my ministry so came to receive healing.

She was progressing quite nicely until one evening a devastating situation came up causing her to again attempt to take her life. We were with her all night at the hospital encouraging her spirit to stay in her body, convincing her spirit that it was not time yet to leave!

She came through that experience. The next time she came to my office for her appointment, she came shuffling through the door. With her head hanging, shoulders drooping, she slumped deep into the chair, and would not even speak.

I encouraged her in the Lord, but was getting no response from her. She just sat there. I felt to ask her, "When are you going to forgive yourself for what happened?"

For the first time she said something. "I could **never** forgive myself!"

At that moment something rose up inside me and I rose off my chair. With my voice raised, I called her by name, saying, "Who do you think you are?"

She was startled because she had never heard me raise my voice. I repeated the question: "Who do you think you are?" No response.

So I said it again, "Who do you think you are? Don't you know God has forgiven you? Haven't you repented?"

"Yes."

"Then God has forgiven you, hasn't He?"

"Yes."

"Well then, who are you to set yourself above God?"

I had never said that before. It was rather a startling statement to my ears as well.

But certainly another consideration is the fact that God forgives. Therefore, if we decide we can't forgive ourselves, we have put ourselves above God, and that is idolatry.

In a sense, we are proud of our ability not to forgive ourselves. After all, that takes real willpower. However, that willpower just may be exerted above even God Himself. And anything we place above God is idolatry.

It is not enough just to ask forgiveness for idolatry. It must be renounced and repented of. We may have even vowed that we would never forgive ourselves. If so, we must renounce that vow and break its power over our lives.

The reason a vow has power is analogous to a train on a track. No matter how much the engineer may want to change direction, the train is committed to the direction the tracks run.

A vow automatically sets the course of our life to fulfill that vow. We must ask God to eradicate those words, so they will not effect our future obedience to forgive.

At this point my friend decided it would be a good thing to forgive herself since our Lord Jesus already paid the price for her forgiveness! May I invite you to pray the following prayer that my friend decided to pray:

Father, in Jesus' name, I repent of and renounce the idolatry of setting myself above God. I repent of and renounce making a vow to never forgive myself.

I ask for and receive Your forgiveness. As an act of my will, I forgive myself for making the vow to never forgive myself, and I release myself from the power of those words.

I choose to love and forgive myself for all the mistakes I have made, for all the foolish things I have said and done.

In Jesus' name. Amen.

14

STUMBLING BLOCKS TO FORGIVENESS

There are three stumbling blocks to forgiveness. They are:

1) I don't feel like it.

2) They don't deserve to be forgiven.

3) I might want to get revenge.

Our son, Jim, stumbled over all three. When he was fifteen, he very graphically demonstrated them.

Jim had a summer job and a motorcycle. One morning he got up early (10:30 a.m.!) to go to the bank to cash his paycheck.

On approaching the bank, Jim saw a car approaching from the opposite direction. It was signaling to turn across Jim's path to go down a side street.

Jim saw the car slowing down preparing to turn, so he moved over into the right-hand lane to get out of its way. But the car didn't stop.

By the time the car turned into and hit Jim, he had moved to the right curb trying to avoid the impact. He was flipped over the car, landing on his head in the middle of the intersection some 20 feet away. Praise God for the helmet on his head. But Jim ended up at the hospital with a badly crushed ankle. (His head was fine!)

A telephone call was put through to me within seconds following the accident. A paramedic was passing by at the moment of the accident and immediately took charge.

By the time Jim arrived at the emergency door of the hospital, I was already there! When he saw me, he quickly assured me he was all right.

"I'm okay, Mom. I was doing fine until that (@#*!%) guy came along."

Upon examination, they determined the need for surgery on the ankle. The doctors picked out as many of the tiny shattered fragments of bone as they could find. Following this, they pinned together the pieces that were large enough to work with. Today Jim still has two steel pins in his ankle.

We were told that Jim probably would never again have full range of motion in that ankle. Also, he probably would have trouble with it for the remainder of his life.

"Probably arthritis will set in very early. It may be very painful to swim." Many other negative reports were spoken that were very hard for an active, six-foot, three-inch fifteen-year-old to hear.

Jim was very angry with the man who hit him. I was also very angry with that man, and had some hard feelings to contend with. I didn't want to consider the possibility of my strapping, healthy, handsome son being crippled the rest of his life.

After a few days of getting settled into the hospital routine, it was time to approach the subject of forgiving.

One day I said, "You know, Jim, we are going to have to deal with what we are feeling inside. We are going to have to deal with the anger and resentment toward that man who hit you."

Guess what Jim said?

"I don't feel like it!"

The number one stumbling block!

I responded, "I know, Jim; I don't feel like it either. But the Bible doesn't say to forgive if we feel like it. It just says to forgive, doesn't it?"

"Yeah, I guess so," he muttered.

Our emotions do come to the forefront in this issue, and certainly they have to be considered. Our feelings may be the fact of the matter, but the Word of God is still the truth of the matter.

So, above our feelings we have to consider what the Word of God says. Does it say we are to forgive if we feel like it? No, it commands us to forgive. There are no conditions.

Forgiving is not a matter of feelings, but of the will. *It is a decision.* We choose. We decide to be obedient to the Word of God and we forgive, just because the Word says forgive.

And so we overcame the number one stumbling block.

And then Jim said, **"But he doesn't deserve to be forgiven."**

The number two stumbling block!

"He saw me! We were eye to eye just before the impact. The sun was shining. I was on a red motorcycle wearing a red helmet. He could have stopped! He doesn't deserve to be forgiven!"

I said, "I know. That's how I feel about it, too, Jim. But we don't have to forgive him just because he deserves it. That really isn't important. We have to forgive him because we deserve it. We don't deserve to hurt the rest of our lives because of what that man did to you. We deserve to be set free in Jesus."

The next day as I walked through Jim's hospital door he greeted me with "O.K. Mom, I'll forgive him -- after we sue."

"Jim!!! We aren't going to sue. We are Christians."

Then I realized stumbling block number three had just surfaced! **I just might want to get revenge!** (And if I forgive, there will be no grounds on which to get revenge.)

Now I'm sure you have never had those kinds of feelings, have you? Christians don't really want to get revenge, do they? But have you ever played around with even the thought of getting even?

Even the thought of how it would feel to get revenge is an open door for the enemy to harass and torment our minds.

I recall from the book of Jeremiah that the Lord really chastened Jeremiah for his thought life. And I said to myself,

"Oh, dear Lord, do I have to bring my thought life under control? After all, no one knows my thoughts except me. My thoughts are my own companions. Do you really mean that You care about my thoughts, too?"

And He responded, "I certainly do."

Let's get some of those thoughts straightened around, lined up with the Word of God:

The mind of those who are out of harmony with God is of little value. (Proverbs 10:20)

Vengeance is mine; I will repay, says the Lord. (Hebrews 10:30)

See that none of you repays another with evil for evil, but always aim to show kindness and seek to do good to all men. (I Thessalonians 5:15)

Even just the thought of getting revenge is an open door for the enemy to harass us, to have a playground in our mind.

Proverbs 10:22 says,

"Don't say 'I will repay evil'; wait for the Lord and He will rescue you."

So we finally worked through the desire for revenge. And then Jim and his mother were able to pray and to release forgiveness from their hearts toward that man.

15

FRUIT OF FORGIVENESS

Almost a year later there was an insurance settlement which provided enough money for Jim to complete his last two years of high school at a military academy. This had been a desire of his heart from the time he was very young.

Isn't it interesting that what the enemy means for harm, God can turn around for our good!

Naturally speaking, Jim was to have problems with the ankle for the rest of his life. But through the accident the way was opened for finances for the military academy. This provided the opportunity for leadership training for Jim to become the man God has called him to be.

When it came time for Jim's physical exam before entering the military academy, we went back to the same doctor who had done the surgery. At the end of the exam Jim asked if he could sign up for football. The doctor's eyes got very big; then he asked Jim if he had experienced any trouble with his ankle.

Jim answered, "No."

The doctor then manipulated Jim's ankle through the full range of motion for a normal ankle and asked if it hurt at all. Again Jim responded, "No."

The doctor then shrugged his shoulders, looked at us in disbelief, and responded, "Why not? Why not let him go out for football!"

Can you imagine Jim doing all the fancy footwork required in playing football? As well as all the marching and standing in formation that is required as part of the routine of a military academy? To think that Jim could ever have done such a thing on an ankle held together with two pins and prayer!

When Jim came home for his first Christmas holiday, we were rehearsing the miracle that God had performed for him. What a miracle to have finances provided to attend the military academy. But an even bigger blessing was the miracle of the healing of his ankle.

We tend to forget the miracles in the common place of our daily routines. As it began to dawn on Jim, his whole countenance began to radiate! Then he jumped up and down on that foot and exclaimed, "Yeah! And it doesn't even hurt!"

I believe the reason Jim had a total healing in that ankle was because he was able to totally forgive, from deep inside his heart, the man who had caused the accident. Hallelujah for the fruit of forgiveness!

16

PREPARING FOR PRAYER

In a moment I want to lead you in a prayer to confess the hurts, anger and resentment you may be experiencing. There may be memories of hurtful situations that have surfaced as I have shared some experiences of my life with you.

Perhaps you are experiencing thoughts and situations that you felt you had already taken care of and forgiven, but they are still gnawing inside you. If you are experiencing an emotional response, this is a good temperature gauge to determine whether an area needs more prayer.

It is important to remember to include specific instances of feelings of rejection in our confession of sin. Rejection leads to anger and resentment, which leads to bitterness and hatred.

This progression defiles not only us, but all those within our sphere of influence (Hebrews 12:15). If a situation is repeated often enough, it will eventually lead to rebellion.

We wonder why we feel rebellious. We wonder why our teenagers are rebellious. We feel rebellious because we are angry. And chances are we are angry because we have felt hurt and rejected by significant people in our lives.

If we are rejected often enough, one of these days we are going to rebel as our way of getting attention. (Recall our definition of rejection: not receiving the love, affirmation, or attention we need at the time we need it, in the way we need it, from the one we need it.)

So when we pray and ask God's forgiveness, remember to include "feeling rejected."

Are you ready for prayer? Let us quiet our minds and hearts. Let us be very specific and focus in on one particularly hurtful or traumatic scene as we pray.

Allow the emotions to surface that you experienced, recognizing them as valid and logical. Remember that as far as emotions are concerned, they are the fact of the matter (Eargle, p 26).

Our interpretation of the facts is sometimes in error. Our perceptions do not necessarily mirror the truth. The Word of God is the truth of the matter. What we are dealing with are facts.

You may even feel as though you have returned to the age you were at the time of the trauma. That is the Lord's way of allowing you to get in touch with your emotions to receive the full healing He has for you.

PRAYER

F *ather, I come to you in the Name of Jesus, confessing my sins according to I John 1:9. I confess the wrong reactions I had toward (name of the one or those who hurt you). I confess the anger, resentment, feelings of being rejected by _____. I felt rejected when they _____. I also felt rejected when they didn't _____. It made me feel hurt, angry, resentful, and bitter. It made me feel (ugly, dumb, stupid, etc.)*

You may add other emotions, such as fear of expressing yourself, fear of confrontation, or fear of their anger. You may also have experienced rage, wrath, hate, thoughts of wanting to kill them or yourself. You may feel inclined to just cry and say, "I hate them, I hate them." This is all part of the cleansing of that emotional wound.

Allow the time for this step to be very thorough. The realization of self-hate may surface at this time, or even resentment toward God. It won't offend Him for you to recognize and confess this. In fact, He already knows it is there, and He is pleased you are willing to admit it.

When you are ready, continue with the prayer:

Father, I receive your forgiveness according to I John 1:9 which says, "If we confess our sins, you are faithful and just to forgive us and to cleanse us from ALL unrighteousness."

I receive your forgiveness, your cleansing, healing, and deliverance. And now that I have it, as an act of my will I choose to pass it on to those who have hurt or offended me.

I forgive (name each one, including God and myself). As an act of my will, I forgive and release each one of us to become the person you have created and called us to be. In the mighty name of Jesus I pray. Amen.

☼ ☼ ☼

Often the above prayer will totally take care of a hurtful memory. However, there may be particularly traumatic situations that specifically need the healing love of Jesus for the hurt to be removed from that painful experience. When this is the case, we should ask can ask Jesus to identify with our hurt and grief and take it to himself. We can do this by inviting the Lord Jesus into that hurtful scene. We can ask him to show us what He would have done if he had been allowed to be the Lord of that situation.

Then we should, through the gifts of the Holy Spirit, ask the Lord to open the eyes of our understanding, as Elijah did in I Kings 6.

In this way, Jesus can totally remove the hurt associated with that painful experience. This won't necessarily wipe out the memory of that experience. It will remove the hurt involved, so that when we reflect back on that scene we will feel totally peaceful (Eargle, p 39). Said in another way, Jesus

86

does not change history but our **perception** of the experience now includes His presence.

God is not the *Author* of all events, but He is the *Master* of all events. This means that nothing has ever happened to you that God cannot and will not use for good if you will surrender it into His hands and allow Him to work (Seamands, p 139).

My love for the Lord has increased tremendously through years of prayer counseling experiences. I have watched Him respond individually according to the needs of each person.

Let me share two examples of the operation of the gift of the word of knowledge. I "saw" Jesus take a young girl to get an ice cream cone. In another instance, I "saw" Him run down the street with a young boy who was feeling rejected by his father. In both examples, I learned only after the fact that these were the very things that meant the most to each child. Only Jesus would have known. I certainly didn't!

God bless you on your journey to becoming whole—physically, emotionally, and spiritually. *May His peace, which passes all understanding, keep your heart and your mind in Christ Jesus. (Philippians 4:7)*

✿ ✿ ✿

And may the God of peace Himself sanctify you through and through -- that is, separate you from profane things, make you pure and wholly consecrated to God -- and may your spirit and soul and body be preserved sound and complete and found blameless at the coming of our Lord Jesus Christ, the Messiah.

Faithful is He who is calling you to Himself and utterly trustworthy, and He will also do it (that is, fulfill His call by hallowing and keeping you). (I Thessalonians 5:23-24 AMP)

STEPS TO FORGIVING

1. RECOGNIZE our hurt and brokenness.

2. CONFESS our wrong reactions.

3. RECEIVE God's forgiveness for yourself.
   A. We cannot give something we have not received.
   B. Christ already paid the price.
   C. Christ made us worthy to be forgiven.

4. FORGIVE and release those who have hurt us.
   A. Forgiving is a decision, not an emotion.
   B. Stumbling blocks to forgiving:
      1. I don't FEEL LIKE it!
      2. They don't DESERVE it!
      3. I just might want to get REVENGE!

5. RELEASE the hurt, resentment, and rejection.
   A. Invite Jesus to be the Lord of that hurtful scene.
   B. Allow Him to express His love to you in the midst of the trauma.

BIBLIOGRAPHY

Adams, Jay E. Competent to Counsel. Grand Rapids: Zondervan, 1970.

Cole, Dr. Edwin. Communication, Sex and Money. Tulsa: Honor Books, 1987.

Eargle, Jon. Healing Where You Hurt...On The Inside. Titusville, FL: Bridge Building Ministries, Inc., 1981.

Frangipane, Francis. A Time To Seek God. Cedar Rapids, IA: Arrow Publications, 1991.

Legamaro, Karen. What is Sin? Tape Series, Part 1. Pheonix, AZ: 1995.

Robinson, Dorothy. Children Of My Soul. Tulsa: Shirley Lamb Ministries, 1965.

Sandford, John and Paula The Transformation of the Inner Man. Tulsa, Victory House, Inc., 1982.

Seamands, David A. Healing for Damaged Emotions. Wheaton, IL: SP Publications, 1983.

Stanley, Charles F. How to Experience Forgiveness. Tape Series, Parts 1,2,3. Atlanta, GA.

Shirley Lamb Ministries

Healing for the Broken-Hearted

1619 E 56TH ST • TULSA, OK 74105 • (918) 747-1662

HEALING THE BROKEN-HEARTED:

- TEACHING BIBLICAL WHOLENESS OF SPIRIT, SOUL, AND BODY

- PRAYER THERAPY

- INDIVIDUAL COUNSELING

- MUSIC THERAPY

- INTEGRATING THE WHOLE PERSON

HELP FOR TRAUMA VICTIMS OF:

- ALCOHOL AND DRUG ABUSE

- DIVORCE

- RAPE

- INCEST

- ACCIDENTS

- ABORTION

- OCCULT INVOLVEMENT

ESTABLISHING RESTORATION
CENTERS FOR TRAUMA VICTIMS BY:

- TEACHING AND MINISTERING WHOLENESS TO A CORE GROUP

- TRAINING THE CORE GROUP TO MINISTER TO OTHERS

SLM FOUNDATION SCRIPTURES:

THE SPIRIT OF THE LORD GOD IS UPON ME BECAUSE THE LORD HAS ANOINTED ME TO PREACH GOOD TIDINGS TO THE MEEK. HE HAS SENT ME TO BIND UP THE BROKEN HEARTED, TO PROCLAIM LIBERTY TO THE CAPTIVES AND THE OPENING OF THE PRISON TO THEM THAT ARE BOUND...

...THAT THEY MIGHT BE CALLED TREES OF RIGHTEOUS-NESS, THE PLANTING OF THE LORD, THAT HE MIGHT BE GLORIFIED....

ISAIAH 61:1-4

MAY YOUR WHOLE SPIRIT, SOUL AND BODY BE KEPT BLAMELESS AT THE COMING OF OUR LORD JESUS CHRIST.
I THESSALONIANS 5:23B (NIV)

ANNOUNCING...

HOW TO BE A PEOPLE HELPER

1. I must first KNOW MYSELF

2. So I can UNDERSTAND OTHERS

3. Before I can HELP ANYONE

Florence Littauer

My popular twelve-week course is now available by correspondence. It is also offered during the Fall and Spring semesters in Tulsa in a three-hour classroom setting on Monday evenings.

Tuition is $40 per four-week session. Estimated cost of required text books is $95. A certificate of completion is awarded.

AGGRESSIVE PRAYERS

A MANUAL FOR VICTORY

Compiled by

SHIRLEY LAMB

This prayer book was birthed out of the crucible of my own prayer life over the past 40 years. Because God is calling His Church into a walk of holiness, we need to pray the Scriptures over ourselves and our loved ones each day. May this manual be a guide into victory in your prayer life!

This 120 page, 5.5x8.5" book is spiral bound so that it can lay flat. It features three sections: Prayers for Others, Personal Prayers, and Famous Prayers.

The
Overcoming
BLOOD

How to defeat today's enemy with God's powerful word

by BOB LAMB

Through a clear, practical analysis of the Scriptures, my husband shows the beneficial relationship between the blood of Jesus and:

† Redemption	† Forgiveness
† Cleansing	† Justification
† Reconciliation	† Sanctification
† True Peace	† Bold Access to God
† Healing	† Eternal Inheritance

Biblical affirmations are given which emphasize the blessings available to every believer through the precious blood of Christ.

Available through **SLM** or your Christian bookstore (ISBN 0-88368-270-2)

Order Form

Shirley Lamb Ministries
1619 E. 56th St.
Tulsa, OK 74105
(918) 747-1662

To:

Ship to (if different address)

QTY.	DESCRIPTION	UNIT PRICE	TOTAL
	AGGRESSIVE PRAYERS - A Manual for Victory	10.00	
	THE OVERCOMING BLOOD by Bob Lamb	7.00	
	PEOPLE HELPING PEOPLE Correspondence Course 12 Lessons, Three Exams. Textbooks ordered separately.	120.00	
	PIANO WORSHIP Cassette of Shirley worshiping God using the piano	10.00	
		SUBTOTAL	
		10% SHIPPING & HANDLING	
		TOTAL DUE	

Sorry, no charge cards, C.O.D. or billing